THE BASICS OF

TENSION

The number of stitches differs depending on the work done firmly or loosely. Referring to the chart on left, choose the crochet hook which is suitable for your work. If your yarn tension is loose, use the hook one size larger than the one indicated in the chart, and if tight, one size smaller.

HOW TO HOLD HOOK AND CAST YARN

Hold the hook in your right hand, at about 4 cm from the top of hook, with the thumb and the forefinger, then attach the middle finger halfway to the top of the hook(see illustration). The middle finger attached leads the yarn on the hook and controls stitch tension. Place the yarn in your left hand between the little finger and the third finger from its outward, cast the shorter end of the yarn on the forefinger from its outward to your side and hold its end with the thumb and the middle finger. Control the yarn casted constantly so that it won't slack.

left hand (casting the yarn)

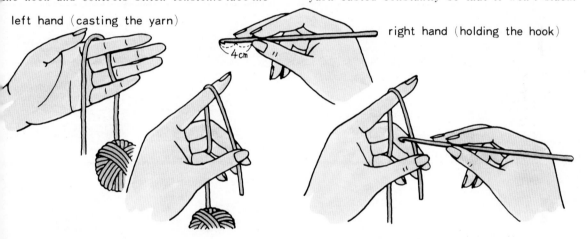

right hand (holding the hook)

4cm

NOW CROCHET IT!

Hold the hook and the yarn comfortably and begin to crochet in a good rhythm. First learn Chain Stitch as any stitching desired may be worked out on this foundation chain.

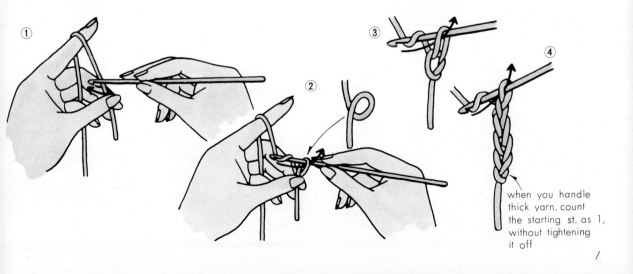

① ② ③ ④

when you handle thick yarn, count the starting st. as 1, without tightening it off

/

SIGNS FOR STITCHES AND ELEMENTARY STITCHES

At the first time, You must memorize these symbolized stitching signs, as any of the patterns in crochet books (published in Japan) are illustrated with them.

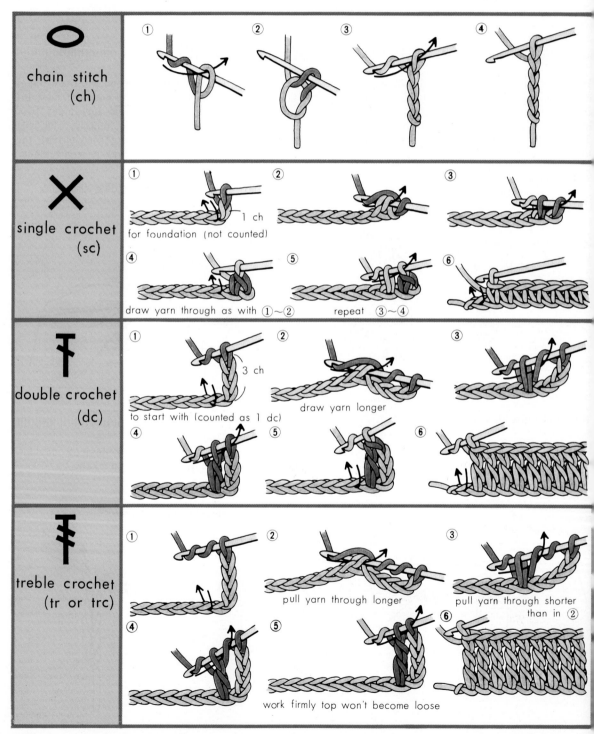

chain stitch (ch)	① ② ③ ④
single crochet (sc)	① 1 ch for foundation (not counted) ② ③ ④ draw yarn through as with ①~② ⑤ repeat ③~④ ⑥
double crochet (dc)	① 3 ch to start with (counted as 1 dc) ② draw yarn longer ③ ④ ⑤ ⑥
treble crochet (tr or trc)	① ② pull yarn through longer ③ pull yarn through shorter than in ② ④ ⑤ work firmly top won't become loose ⑥

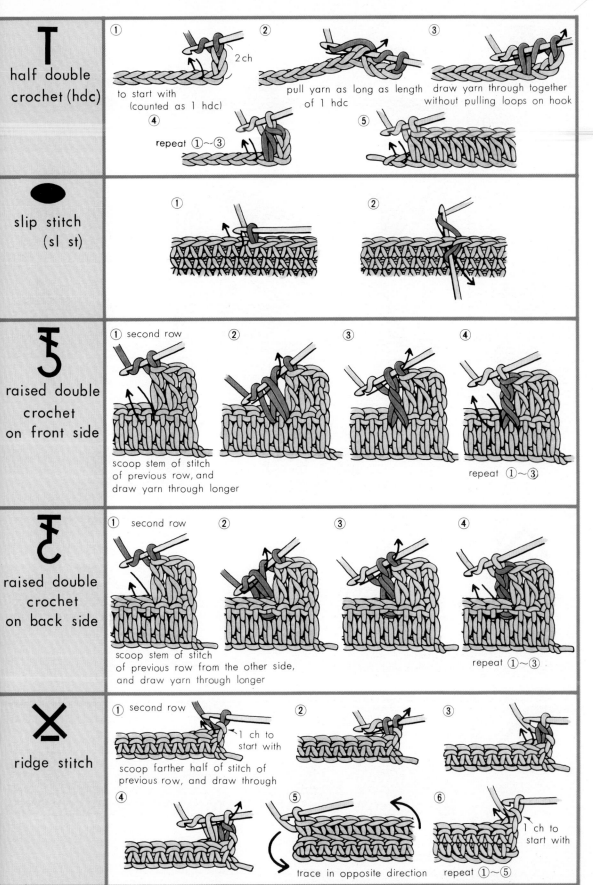

half double crochet (hdc)

① to start with (counted as 1 hdc) 2 ch
② pull yarn as long as length of 1 hdc
③ draw yarn through together without pulling loops on hook
④ repeat ①~③
⑤

slip stitch (sl st)

①
②

raised double crochet on front side

① second row
②
③
④
scoop stem of stitch of previous row, and draw yarn through longer
repeat ①~③

raised double crochet on back side

① second row
②
③
④
scoop stem of stitch of previous row from the other side, and draw yarn through longer
repeat ①~③

ridge stitch

① second row   1 ch to start with
scoop farther half of stitch of previous row, and draw through
②
③
④
⑤ trace in opposite direction
⑥ 1 ch to start with
repeat ①~⑤

3

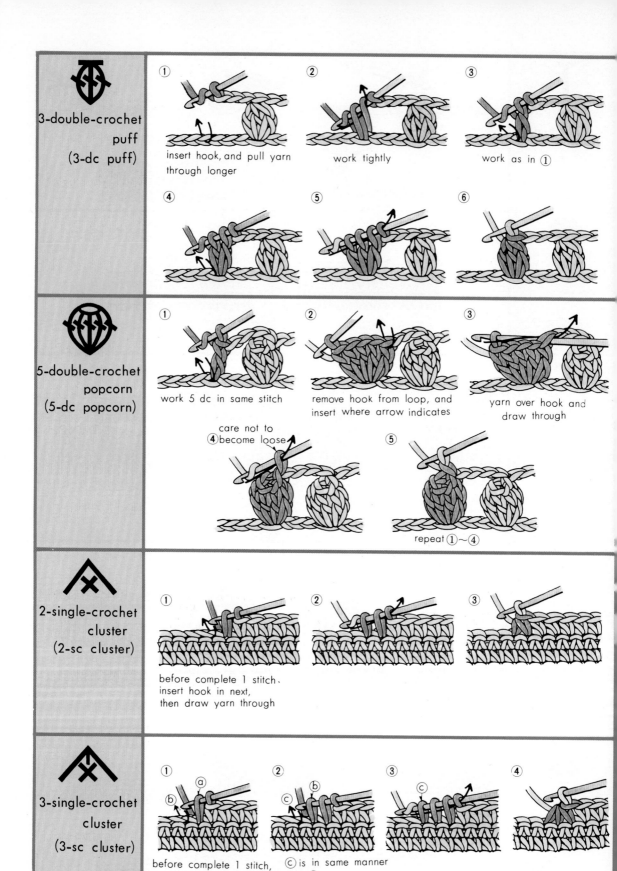

3-double-crochet puff (3-dc puff)

① insert hook, and pull yarn through longer
② work tightly
③ work as in ①
④
⑤
⑥

5-double-crochet popcorn (5-dc popcorn)

① work 5 dc in same stitch
② remove hook from loop, and insert where arrow indicates
③ yarn over hook and draw through
④ care not to become loose
⑤ repeat ①~④

2-single-crochet cluster (2-sc cluster)

① ② ③
before complete 1 stitch, insert hook in next, then draw yarn through

3-single-crochet cluster (3-sc cluster)

① ② ③ ④
before complete 1 stitch, insert hook in next, and draw yarn through ⓑ
ⓒ is in same manner as ①

2-double-crochet cluster (2-dc cluster)

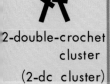

① insert hook as arrow indicates, and draw yarn through

② insert hook as indicated, and draw yarn through

③ 2 dc on hook in same length, and draw yarn through at a time

2-single-crochet Increase (2-sc inc.)

① insert hook as indicated, and draw yarn through

3-single-crochet increase (3-sc inc.)

  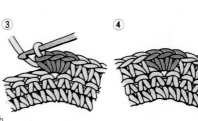

① insert hook as indicated, and draw yarn through

② hook into same stitch, and draw yarn through

3-double-crochet increase (3-dc inc.)

② work dc in same stitch

③ 3 dc in same length

3-chain picot (3-ch picot)

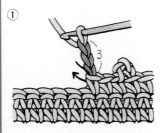 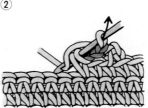 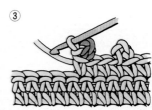

slip stitch on top of the sc

5

● SCOOPING FARTHER HALF AND BACK OF THE STITCH

This keeps the base of the first row finished firm and does not allow the chain loosen. When you trace back, the first row will be made neatly.

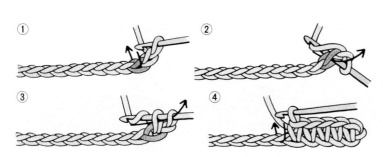

● SCOOPING BACK OF THE STITCH

This makes the foudation chain look natural.

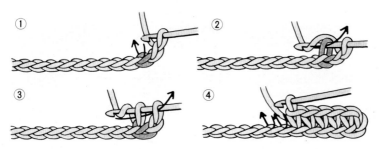

● WITH SINGLE CROCHET

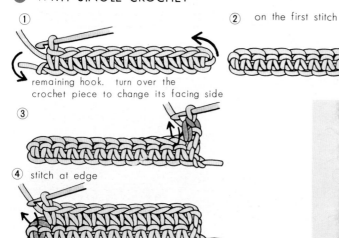

① remaining hook. turn over the crochet piece to change its facing side

② on the first stitch — 1 ch to start with

③

④ stitch at edge

①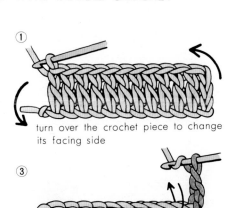

turn over the crochet piece to change
its facing side

②

3 ch to start with

③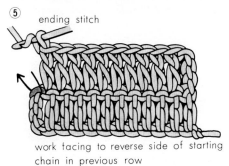

④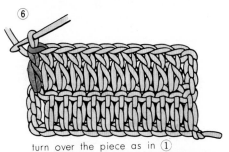

⑤

ending stitch

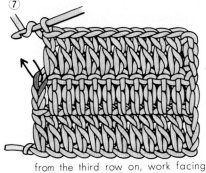

work facing to reverse side of starting
chain in previous row

⑥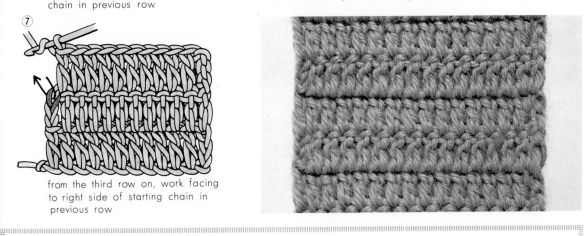

turn over the piece as in ①

⑦

from the third row on, work facing
to right side of starting chain in
previous row

STARTING CHAIN AND THE HEIGHT OF STITCHES

At the beginning of every row, you work
a chain up to the height of the stitch which
makes the height of row. We call this chain
"Starting Chain". Compared, the height of
each stitch will be shown in the chart (right).

single crochet

half double crochet

double crochet

treble crochet

3-loops on hook

This is the method of starting from its center working in a ring, and is mostly used for making motifs or hats. Here is the most popular example.

● MAKING RING WITH END OF YARN

With the yarn doubled, the center will be tighten - ed firm. If yarn end is finished neatly, the piece of work will look more beautiful.

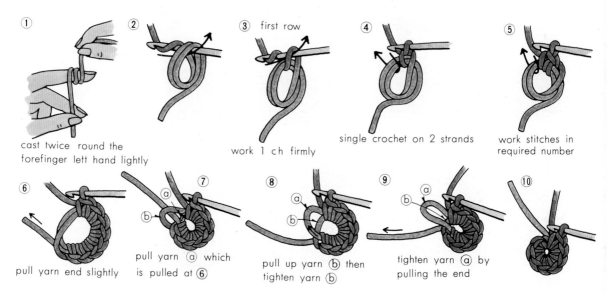

① cast twice round the forefinger lett hand lightly ② work 1 ch firmly ③ first row ④ single crochet on 2 strands ⑤ work stitches in required number

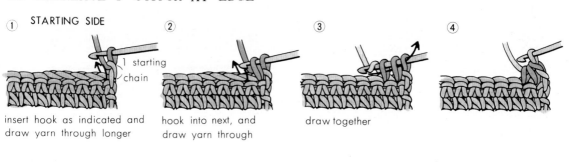

⑥ pull yarn end slightly ⑦ pull yarn ⓐ which is pulled at ⑥ ⑧ pull up yarn ⓑ then tighten yarn ⓑ ⑨ tighten yarn ⓐ by pulling the end ⑩

||||||||||||||||||||||||||| **TO DECREASE STITCHES** |||||||||||||||||||||||||||

● SINGLE CROCHET

TO DECREASE 1 STITCH AT EDGE

① STARTING SIDE — 1 starting chain / insert hook as indicated and draw yarn through longer
② hook into next, and draw yarn through
③ draw together
④

⑤ ENDING SIDE / insert hook in second from edge, and draw yarn through
⑥ hook into edge stitch, and draw yarn through a little longer
⑦ draw together
⑧ work ⓐ firmly, ⓑ loosely

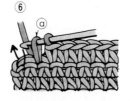
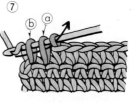
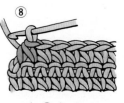

TO DECREASE 2 STITCHES OR MORE AT EDGE

ENDING LAST STITCH

① make loop of last stitch
larger, then yarn through

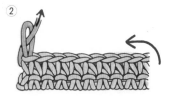

② tighten by pulling yarn
through, and turn over
the crochet piece

CARRYING YARN ACROSS

③ hook into the stitch, omitting
stitches to be decreased,
and draw yarn through

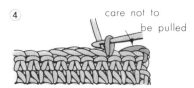

care not to
be pulled

④ slip stitch into next without
pulling the yarn carried across

⑤ single crochet on

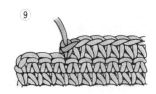

slip stitch

stitches omitted

⑥

ENDING SIDE

to be
decreased

⑦ slip stitch on the stitch before

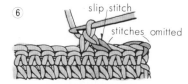

⑧ make loop on hook larger,
and end as in ①〜②

⑨

● DOUBLE CROCHET
TO DECREASE 1 STITCH AT EDGE

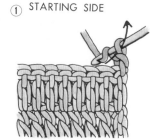

① STARTING SIDE

to start with,
3 ch loosely

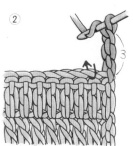

②

hook into next, and
draw yarn through

③

④

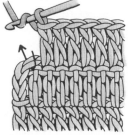

⑤ ENDING SIDE

hook into second stitch
from edge (arrow),
and work half of dc

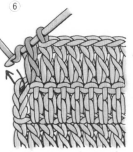

⑥

hook into stitch on edge
(starting chain previous row),
and draw yarn through

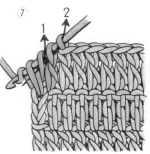

⑦

draw yarn through all
loops on hook at a time 2

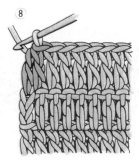

⑧

TO DECREASE 2 STITCHES OR MORE AT EDGE

① STARTING SIDE

1 sc into second

②

1 hdc into third firmly,
then into fourth normally

③

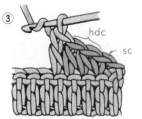

hdc

sc

work stitch by stitch changing
their length so that the edge
will be made slopewise

④ ENDING SIDE

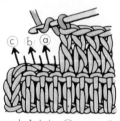

work 1 hdc ⓐ normally,
ⓑ firmly then 1 sc ⓒ

⑤

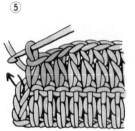

end by working sl st
into edge

⑥

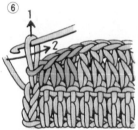

1

2

make loop larger, and
draw yarn through to
end off

⑦

care not to
be pulled

1 sl st into next without
pulling the yarn carried
over

 TO INCREASE STITCHES

● SINGLE CROCHET

TO INCREASE 1 SC ON EDGE

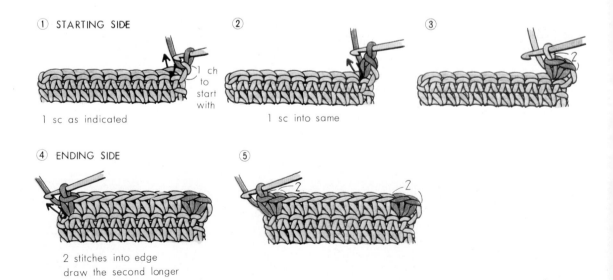

① STARTING SIDE

1 ch
to
start
with

1 sc as indicated

②

1 sc into same

③

2

④ ENDING SIDE

2 stitches into edge
draw the second longer

⑤

2

2

TO INCREASE 2 STITCHES OR MORE ON EDGE

① STARTING SIDE

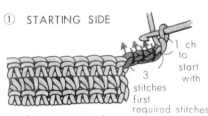

1 ch to start with

3 stitches first required stitches

work out starting chain, and 1 sc

②

3 ch as required

③ ENDING SIDE

pull yarn through edge stitch

④

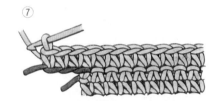

work starting chain for increase

⑤

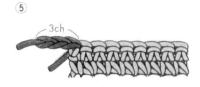

3ch

⑥

work sc on

⑦

● DOUBLE CROCHET

TO INCREASE 1 STITCH ON EDGE

① STARTING SIDE

3 ch to start with

hook into edge stitch and draw yarn through

②

1

2

1 dc

③

2 dc

④ ENDING SIDE

2 dc into edge stitch (starting in previous row)

⑤

1

2

make second stitch longer

⑥

2

2

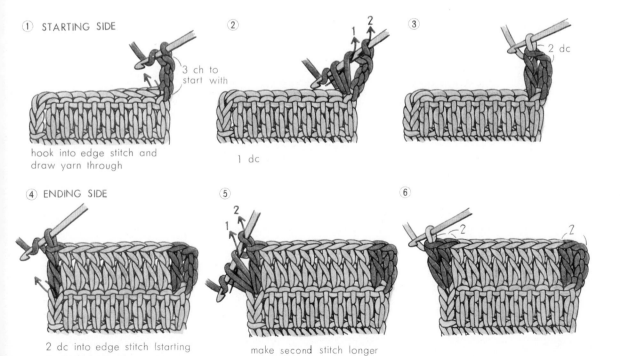

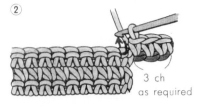

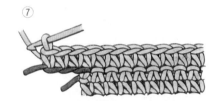

TO INCREASE BY WORKING OUT A CHAIN

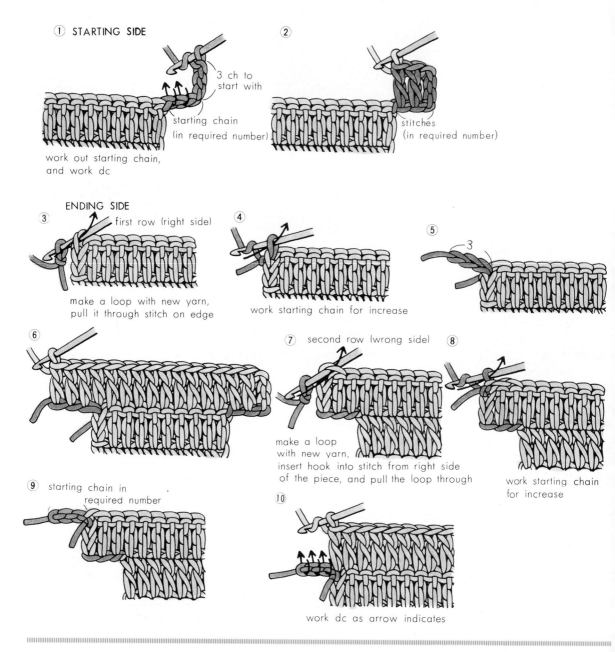

① STARTING SIDE

3 ch to start with

starting chain (in required number)

work out starting chain, and work dc

②

stitches (in required number)

ENDING SIDE

③ first row (right side)

make a loop with new yarn, pull it through stitch on edge

④ work starting chain for increase

⑤ 3

⑥

⑦ second row (wrong side) ⑧

make a loop with new yarn, insert hook into stitch from right side of the piece, and pull the loop through

work starting chain for increase

⑨ starting chain in required number

⑩

work dc as arrow indicates

YARN: RELEASING AND WINDING

Most knitting yarns sold in shops are in the form of ball or skein. Those yarns therefore have to be kept in the correct form ready to be used.

1. The Yarn Balled

Use as it is shown in the illustration by drawing yarn end from the hole at its center. Retain the paper belt wrapped around until the yarn is used up. This will keep the yarn from tangling itself and at the same time you can conveniently get the yarn, if needed more, corresponding to the mark on the belt.

2. The Yarn Skeined

It would be helpful if you have some tools for releasing yarns from skeins but if you have none, ask someone to hang skein on hands in the way as is shown in the illustration and wind it into ball. But be sure wind the yarn loosely.

If you crochet at home, better to have the yarn released instead balled, in a box neatly, and when the whole yarn released push slightly downward with your palm so that the yarn won't tangle itself. Thus the best way to keep the yarn without its ball rolling or being pulled.

● WHEN MAKE A NEW ROW

When you use two colors, work every 2 rows without turning its facing side. The yarn is carried across at the edge of the crochet piece.

①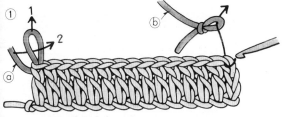

tighten through yarn ⓐ attach yarn ⓑ

②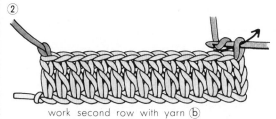

work second row with yarn ⓑ

③

change the yarn with the last stitch of the second row

④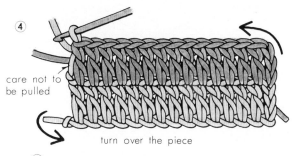

care not to be pulled

turn over the piece

⑤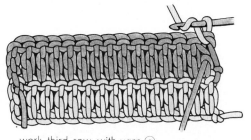

work third row with yarn ⓐ

⑥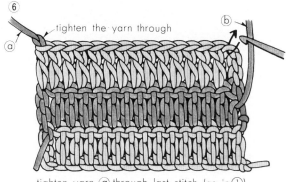

tighten the yarn through

tighten yarn ⓐ through last stitch (as in ①) hook into, and pull out yarn ⓑ

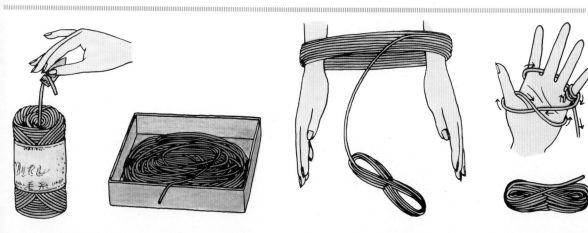

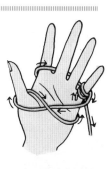

● DURING THE COURSE OF WORK: WRAPPING UP WITH NEW COLOR

This is the method carrying over new yarn during the course of work,   and is suitable for small succeeding patterns. The wrong side of the piece is neatly finished.

①

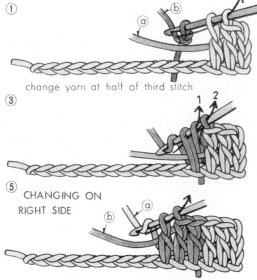

change yarn at half of third stitch

③

⑤ CHANGING ON RIGHT SIDE

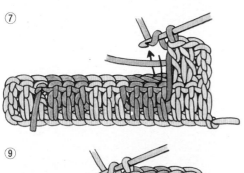

leave yarn ⓑ aside at half of stitch
put yarn ⓐ on the wrong side of yarn ⓑ

⑦

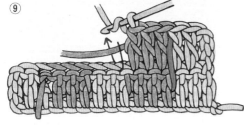

⑨

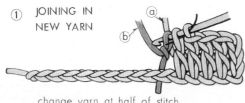

● INTERSECTION

This method is to join new colors in each pattern of the work by making an intersection with the yarn next on the wrong side of the piece.

① JOINING IN NEW YARN

change yarn at half of stitch

② WRAPPING UP

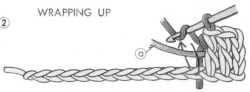

carry yarn ⓐ crosswise, wrap it up with yarn ⓑ

④

⑥ CHANGING ON WRONG SIDE
(starting side)

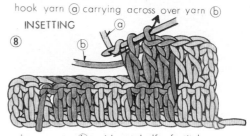

hook yarn ⓐ carrying across over yarn ⓑ

INSETTING

⑧

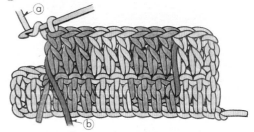

leave yarn ⓑ aside at half of stitch
hook ⓐ from your side of ⓑ

⑩ EDGE (ending side)

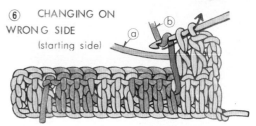

change yarn to ⓐ as in ⑧ , and leave aside yarn ⓑ on your side

The yarn changed is carried over lengthwise. Is good to be used on the edges of large patterns, bold stripes, and one-point patterns.

②

work forward with yarn ⓑ

③

change yarn as in ①, and
work toward with yarn ⓒ

⑤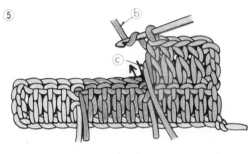

④ CHANGING ON
   WRONG SIDE

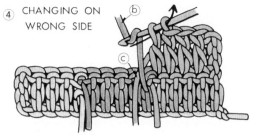

leave yarn ⓒ aside on your side of the piece
hook yarn ⓑ from your side of ⓒ

⑥ CHANGING ON
   RIGHT SIDE

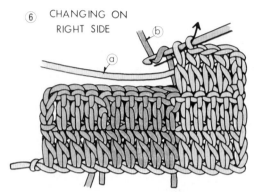

leave yarn ⓐ aside, hook yarn ⓑ
carrying across farther side of ⓐ

⑦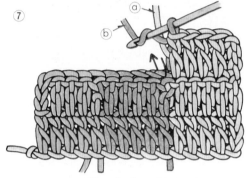

carry yarn ⓐ to farther side work
forward with ⓑ

⑧ RIGHT SIDE

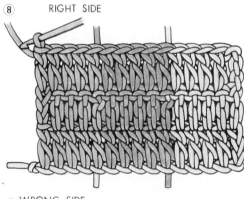

⑨ WRONG SIDE

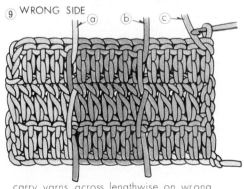

carry yarns across lengthwise on wrong
side, change color making intersection

RIGHT SIDE

WRONG SIDE

This is the way of joining crochet pieces stitch to stitch. Use any of the following methods according to the thickness of yarn, the work whether finished firmly or in a lightweight pattern, and the kind where to be used. Using right method on right place is the key to keep the crochet piece in a good shape longer.

If the yarn end is left on the edge of the crochet piece, cut off the end leaving the yarn joining.

● DARNING STITCH BY STITCH Place right side up, and join by matching the seams.

①
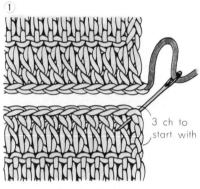
3 ch to start with

scoop 2 strands of chain

②
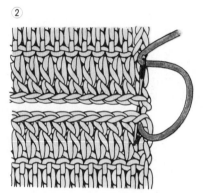

scoop whole top of first stitch the other side, same stitch as in 1 this side, then tighten yarn

③

from second stitch, scoop from farther side to your side, stitch by stitch, matchig seams together, and fasten yarn each time

④
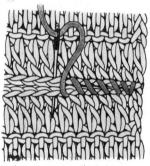

tighten yarn so that seams become as flat as other part of the piece

● SCOOP-DARNING Place right sides of the crochet piece up, and join by matching the seams.

①

3 ch to start with

scoop 2 strands of chain

②
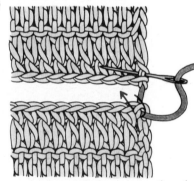

scoop between top and stem the other side, 1 loop between first and second stitches and 1 strand of chain this side

③
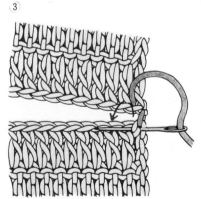

scoop the other side in same manner as first stitch

④
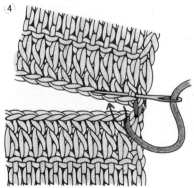

from second stitch this side, scoop in same manner as the other side

⑤

tighten yarn stitch by stitch taking care of balancing

ASSEMBLING

This is a method used for joining side seams or row edges. Using right method at right place is important to finish the crochet work beautiful and to keep it in a good shape longer. Therefore you have to pick up any of the following methods according to the work eith-er it's finished in a complicated pattern or a simple pattern, the seam where to be sewn to the side seams of side, under-sleeve, armhole, etc. The yarn for joining has to be taken before the foundation chain is worked out.

● FINISHED IN SLIP STITCH

Joined firmly but has little stretch, this method is suitable for arm seams. Not good for softly finished work or the work which has some slackness. And also the work made of heavy yarn is better to avoid, for its seam may become bulky. Be careful that the stitches not to be worked out too firmly.

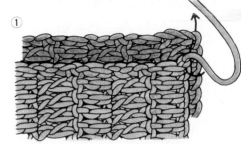

① put pieces right sides together
hook into starting stitch on edge
(arrow) and draw yarn through firmly

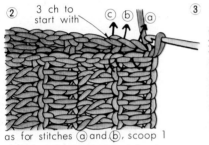

② 3 ch to start with

as for stitches ⓐ and ⓑ, scoop 1 strand each on edge, and for the stitch ⓒ the other side, scoop 2 strands, then slip stitch

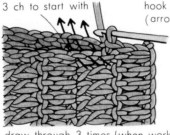

③ 3 ch to start with

draw through 3 times (when work dc) for each row

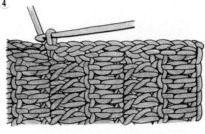

④

● FINISHED IN CHAIN STITCH

This is the simplest method commonly used for side seams or under-sleeve seams. Join top of the row together with single crochet or slip stitch, pass across each of the row by working chain stitch as long as the height of the row. The number of the stitches differs depending on the height of row.

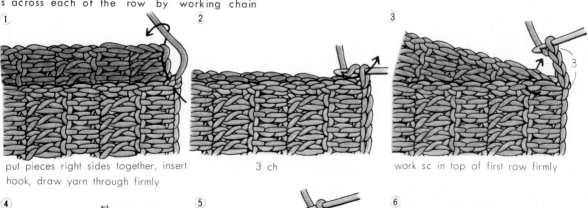

① put pieces right sides together, insert hook, draw yarn through firmly

② 3 ch

③ work sc in top of first row firmly

④ 2 ch from second stitch

⑤ 1 sc in top of second row

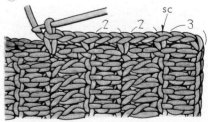

⑥ join together every row with sc

● FINISHED IN SCOOPING UP

The seams finished smooth so this method is commonly
used for the work double crochet or mesh.

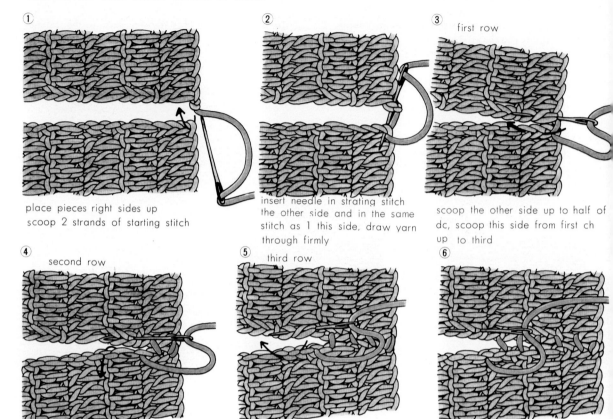

① place pieces right sides up
scoop 2 strands of starting stitch

② insert needle in strating stitch
the other side and in the same
stitch as 1 this side, draw yarn
through firmly

③ first row
scoop the other side up to half of
dc, scoop this side from first ch
up to third

④ second row
scoop the other side second stitch from
top of previous row, and this side from
half of dc up to top of next row

⑤ third row
scoop in same manner as first row
scoop stitches without splitting yarn
of the piece, draw yarn through stitch
by stitch

⑥ repeat ④~⑤

● FINISHED IN BACK STITCH

This is a method suitable for the work when joining curved or sloped seams to straight seams, or
when joining works while either side of the seams has to be tucked in some easiness. Used for
joinig arm seams, designed seams, and for joining
rows and stitches. Scoop roughly so that the
work be finished naturally.

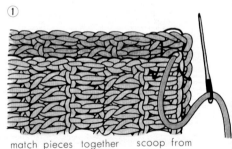

① match pieces together   scoop from
starting stitch up to half of first row

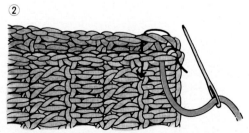

② scoop from same stitch as 1 up to
top of first row

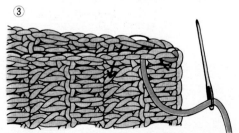

③ scoop from center of first row up to
that of second

● FINISHED IN OVERCAST

When all of the motifs have been made, place them in lines following their shape and begin to join. Having finished each of the lines crosswise, join lengthwise.

①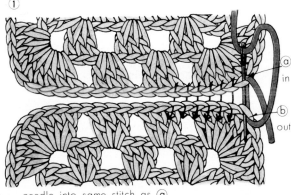

ⓐ in
ⓑ out

needle into same stitch as ⓐ

assemble stitch by stitch by casting yarn right to left

draw yarn each time of stitching

② second piece

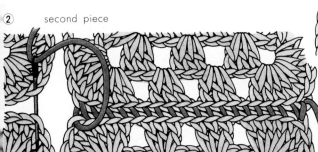

scoop stitch on corner of second piece, join in same manner as ①

③

carry yarn across between pieces first and second

④ ⑤

rst piece is joined in same
anner as ①, ②
t corner, scoop same stitch
s ③

yarn is crossed on corner
right side

● PICKING UP STITCHES FROM THE ROW EDGE ; SPLITTING INTO EDGE STITCH

Used in case of the yarn heavier than the worsted weight, the work will be finished neatly.

WORKING IN SINGLE CROCHET

WORKING IN DOUBLE CROCHET

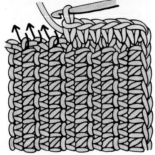

Work single crochet splitting into the stitch on the edge but on the foundation row, pick up 1 chain stitch directly.

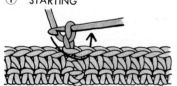

Pick up stitches splitting into stitch on edge.

● BACK SINGLE CROCHET

Here is the method most commonly used to make the edge work look neat. Learn the correct way of ending last stitch, finishing yarn end especially at the begininng of the work and at the ending of the work.

① STARTING

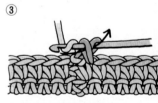

work 1 ch to start with, turn tip of hook your side, scoop last stitch of previons row

②

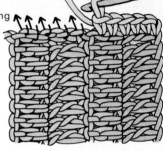

③

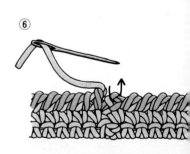

in same manner as sc

④

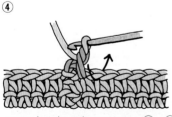

toward right side repeating ②~④

⑤ ENDING LAST STITCH

cut yarn end leaving 6~7 cm, draw through (arrow)

⑥

⑦

⑧ FINISHING YARN END (wrong side)

needle into stitches on wrong side from first stitch, carry yarn end through

● BUTTONHOLE (IN SINGLE CROCHET, HORIZONTAL)

①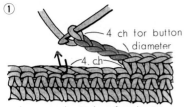
4 ch for button diameter
4 ch
make enough stitches for diameter of the button, then 1 sc into next stitch

②

③
4 sc, scooping chain

④

⑤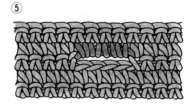

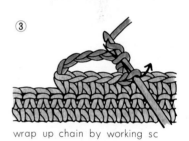

● BUTTON LOOP (IN SINGLE CROCHET)

①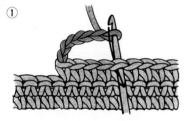

②
join in slip stitch

③
wrap up chain by working sc

④
hook as indicated, and work slip stitch

⑤
continue in sc

● BUTTON LOOP (THREAD LOOP)

①

②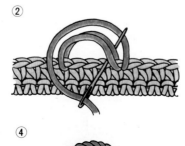

③

④

21

THE BASICS OF KNITTING

● USING KNITTING NEEDLES

This is a method used for stockinet stitches, and also to make foundation rib, as it provides neat finish and elasticity. Very popular and easiest for beginners.

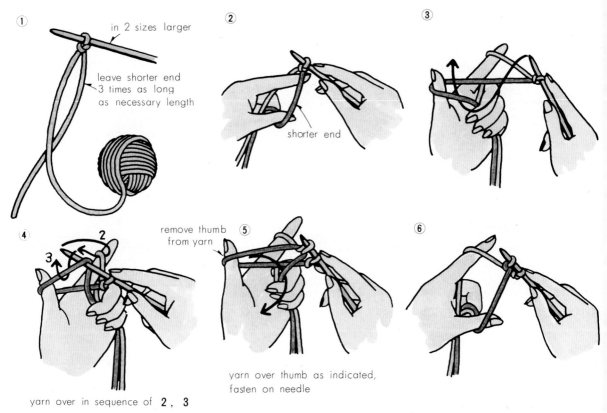

① in 2 sizes larger

leave shorter end 3 times as long as necessary length

② shorter end

③

④ yarn over in sequence of **2 , 3**

⑤ remove thumb from yarn

yarn over thumb as indicated, fasten on needle

⑥

● USING A HOOK

This method is free from running out or leaving over of the yarn. It forms a chain on one side by casting the yarn as shown below. Later **make-up** is not necessary, and the edge does not stretch.

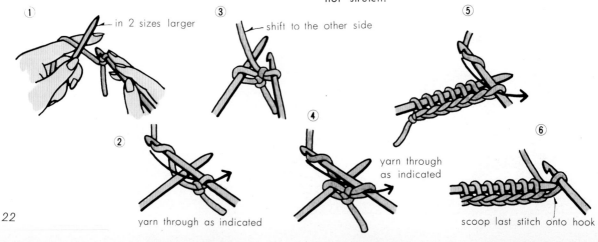

① in 2 sizes larger

② yarn through as indicated

③ shift to the other side

④ yarn through as indicated

⑤

⑥ scoop last stitch onto hook

● STITCHES ABLE TO BE UNKNITTED

Stitches are made by picking up a loop from the chain which has been worked in separate yarn. Used to work in rib (ribbing) on the ends of sleeves or hem. Also adaptable in case of running out of yarn.

① foundation chain in separate yarn

scoop back stitches of chain

②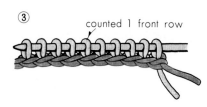
yarn through as indicated

③ 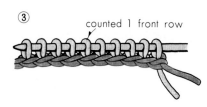 counted 1 front row

④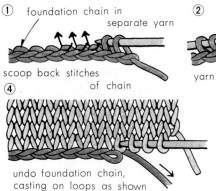
undo foundation chain, casting on loops as shown

● SINGLE RIB (RIBBING)

This method is not only easy to work but also provides a neat finish. Has fine elasticity, and is ideal for thick, bulky yarn (to make socks, for example). The first and seconds rows will be made in French Stitching (shown below, ⑥ & ⑦) then alternate stitching, single ribbing as called, will continue from 3rd row.

①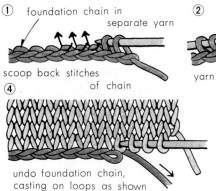
yarn on needle as indicated

②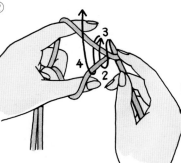
continue in sequence 2 ~ 4

③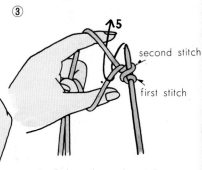
second stitch
first stitch
make 3rd stitch as show 5

④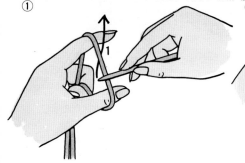
repeat case ②

⑤
repeat ③, ④ until desired number of stitches will be made

⑥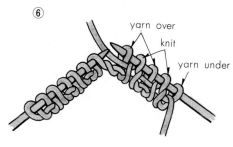
yarn over
knit
yarn under
slip off first stitch. knit and pass stitches as shown (passing is made by shifting stitch on front of knitting piece)

⑦
pass 1 stitch as in case of previous row. repeat knit and pass, thus working french stitching

⑧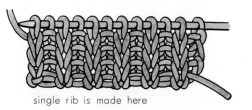
single rib is made here

● DOUBLE RIB (RIBBING)

This method is **also** to be recommended if neatness and elasticity are required. When you try this, be sure you've mastered **single** rib.

①~⑦ starting stitches are in the multiple number of 4 plus 2, as in case of single rib

⑧

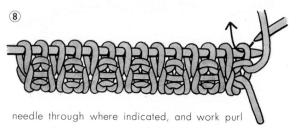

needle through where indicated, and work purl

⑨

remove following stitch, leave it unworked, and continue purl with 3rd stitch

⑩

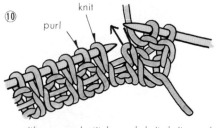

with removed stitch work knit, knit again and purl

⑪

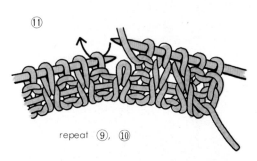

repeat ⑨, ⑩

⑫

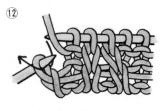

end with purl as indicated

⑬

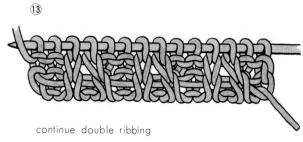

continue double ribbing

‖‖‖‖‖‖‖‖‖‖‖‖‖‖‖‖‖‖‖‖‖‖‖‖‖‖‖ CORRECT WAY TO HOLD
NEEDLES AND YARN ‖‖‖‖‖‖‖‖‖‖‖‖‖‖‖‖‖‖‖‖‖‖‖‖‖‖‖‖‖‖‖‖

Yarn may be taken either on your left hand or right hand. The easier for you, the better.

ON LEFT HAND

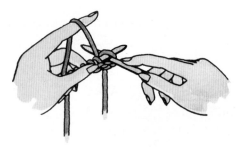

ON RIGHT HAND

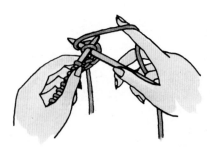

SIGNS FOR STITCHES AND ELEMENTARY STITCHES

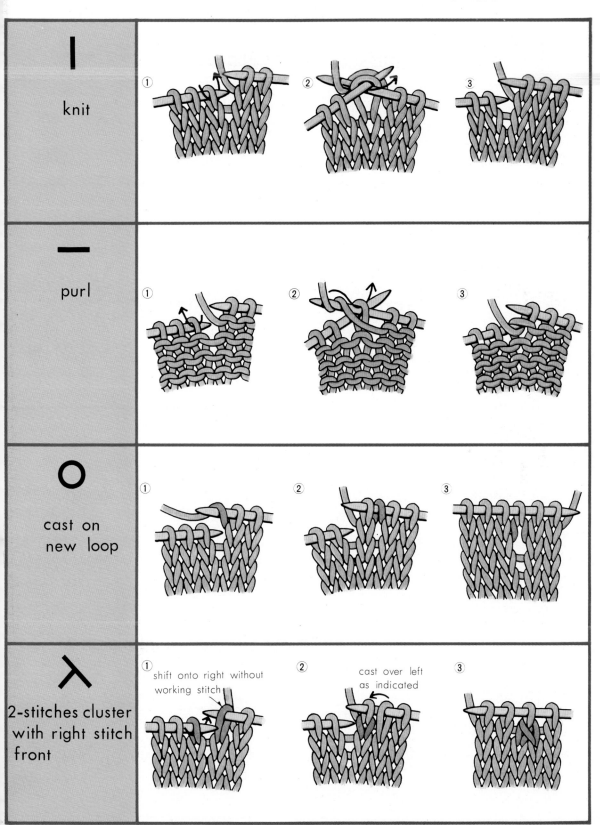

l knit	① ② ③
— purl	① ② ③
O cast on new loop	① ② ③
⋋ 2-stitches cluster with right stitch front	① shift onto right without working stitch ② cast over left as indicated ③

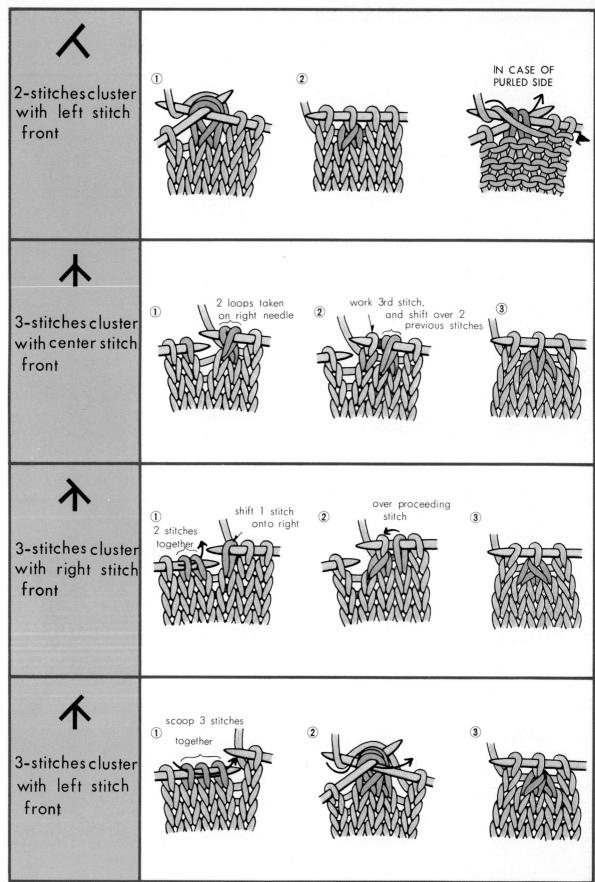

2-stitches cluster with left stitch front

① ② IN CASE OF PURLED SIDE

3-stitches cluster with center stitch front

① 2 loops taken on right needle ② work 3rd stitch, and shift over 2 previous stitches ③

3-stitches cluster with right stitch front

① 2 stitches together shift 1 stitch onto right ② over proceeding stitch ③

3-stitches cluster with left stitch front

① scoop 3 stitches together ② ③

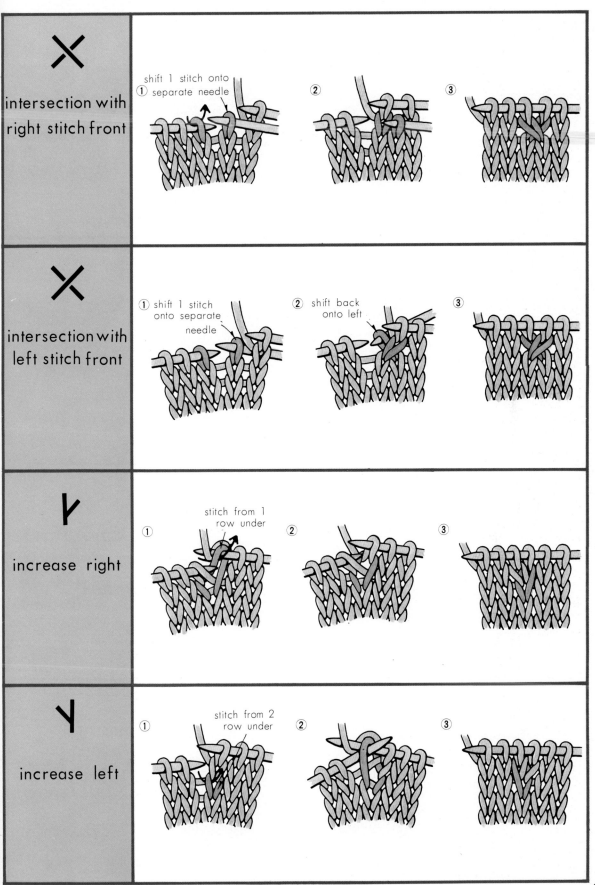

✕ intersection with right stitch front	① shift 1 stitch onto separate needle ② ③
✕ intersection with left stitch front	① shift 1 stitch onto separate needle ② shift back onto left ③
Ɣ increase right	① stitch from 1 row under ② ③
Ɣ increase left	① stitch from 2 row under ② ③

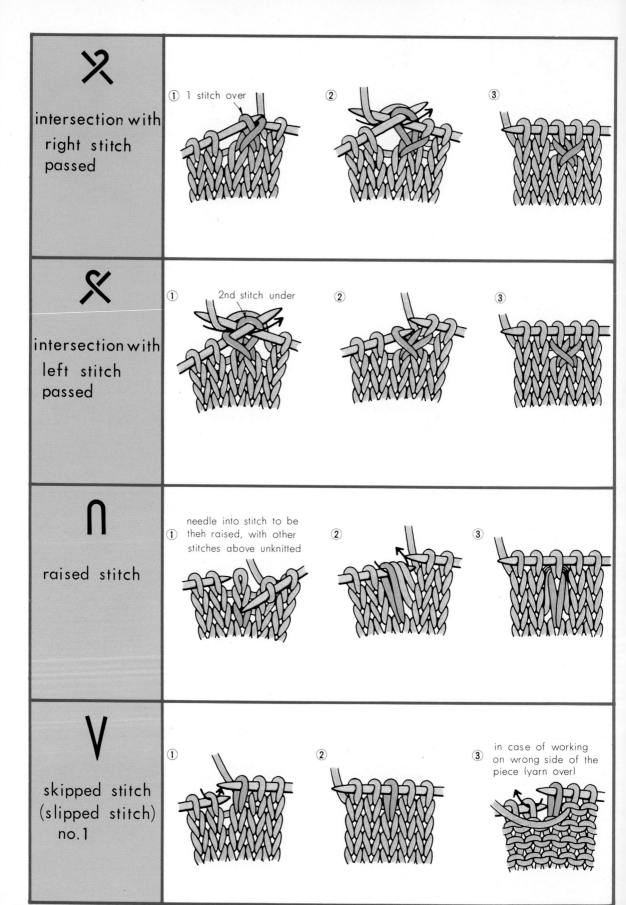

⤬ **intersection with right stitch passed**	① 1 stitch over ② ③
⤬ **intersection with left stitch passed**	① 2nd stitch under ② ③
⋂ **raised stitch**	① needle into stitch to be theh raised, with other stitches above unknitted ② ③
V **skipped stitch (slipped stitch) no.1**	① ② ③ in case of working on wrong side of the piece (yarn over)

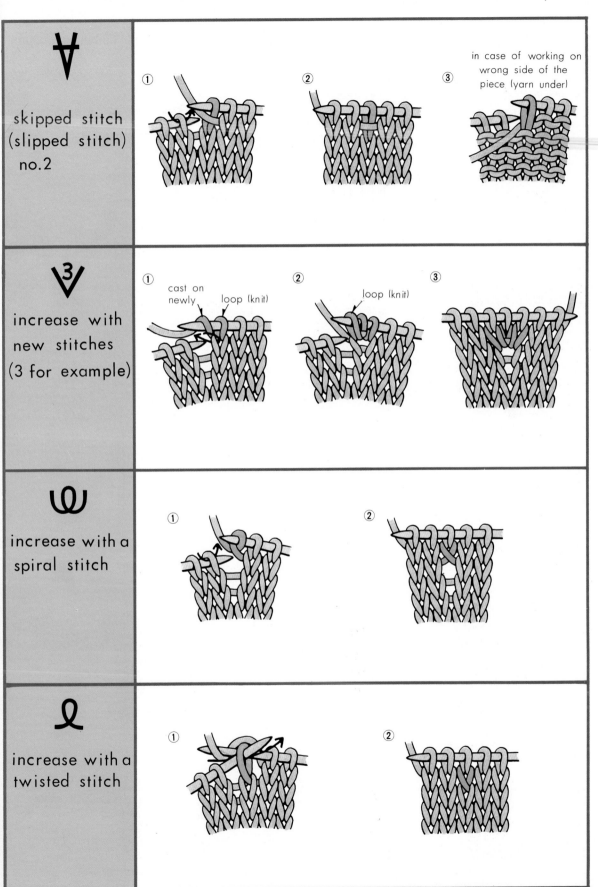

skipped stitch
(slipped stitch)
no.2

① ② ③ in case of working on wrong side of the piece (yarn under)

increase with
new stitches
(3 for example)

① cast on newly   loop (knit)   ② loop (knit)   ③

increase with a
spiral stitch

① ②

increase with a
twisted stitch

① ②

The illustrations below are the most popular knitted pieces. The first two, Stockinet Stitches, are made in knit on front and purl on back. The Garter, Single Rib and Double Rib are also of frequent use.

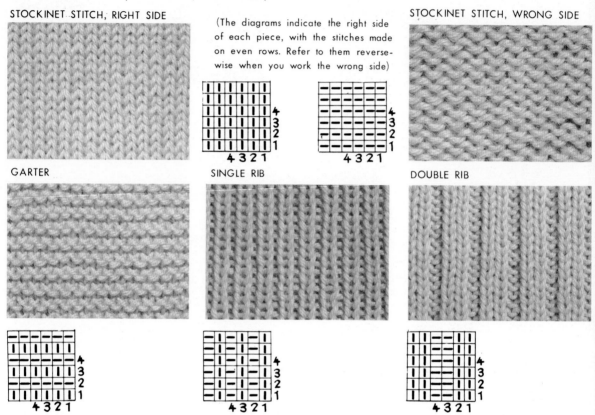

STOCKINET STITCH, RIGHT SIDE

(The diagrams indicate the right side of each piece, with the stitches made on even rows. Refer to them reverse-wise when you work the wrong side)

STOCKINET STITCH, WRONG SIDE

GARTER

SINGLE RIB

DOUBLE RIB

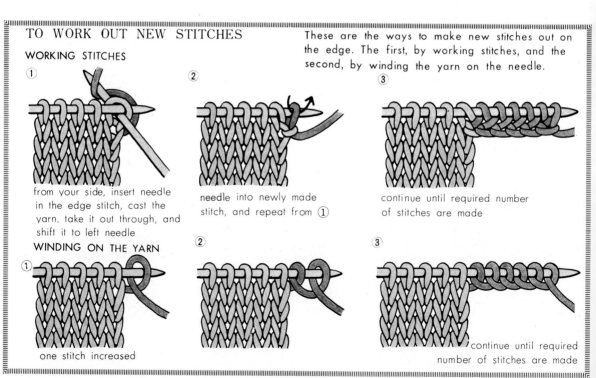

TO WORK OUT NEW STITCHES

These are the ways to make new stitches out on the edge. The first, by working stitches, and the second, by winding the yarn on the needle.

WORKING STITCHES

① from your side, insert needle in the edge stitch, cast the yarn, take it out through, and shift it to left needle

② needle into newly made stitch, and repeat from ①

③ continue until required number of stitches are made

WINDING ON THE YARN

① one stitch increased

②

③ continue until required number of stitches are made

TO DECREASE STITCHES

Important is to avoid loosening the tension that leads to stretching the edge stitches. The following are examples of decreasing stitches. Please choose one that suits for later grafting.

● TO DECREASE AT THE EDGE

RIGHT END

① (EXTREME RIGHT)

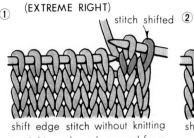

stitch shifted

②

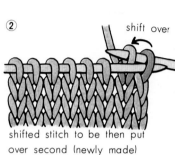

shift over

shift edge stitch without knitting to right, and work second-from-edge stitch

shifted stitch to be then put over second (newly made) stitch

③

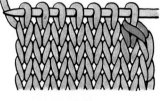

(EXTREME LEFT)

①

②

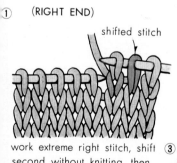

after knitting third-from-edge stitch, scoop 2 left stitches to knit together

LEFT END

● TO DECREASE IN THE COURSE (WITH SECOND-FROM-EDGE STITCHES)

① (RIGHT END)

shifted stitch

②

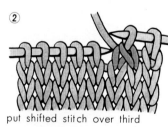

put shifted stitch over third

work extreme right stitch, shift second without knitting, then work third

③

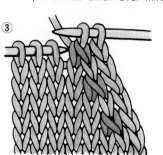

EXTREME RIGHT

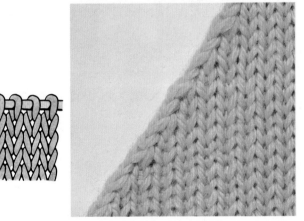

31

① (LEFT END)

after knitting third-from-edge stitch, scoop following 2 stitches with left on front, and knit together

②

knit extreme stitch

③

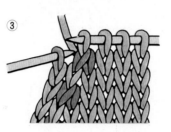

LEFT END

● TO DECREASE 2 STITCHES OR MORE AT THE EDGE

① (EXTREME RIGHT)

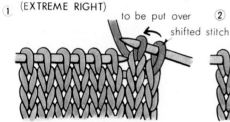

to be put over
shifted stitch

shift extreme right stitch without knittng, knit second-from-edge stitch

②

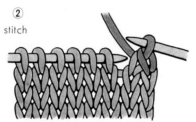

put shifted stitch over newly made stitch

③

continue repeating from 1 until required number of stitches are decreased

RIGHT END   LEFT END

TENSION OR GAUGE

Tension bears the rate of the number of rows and stitches within a certain square measure. Tension is usually on a sample of 10 square centimeters. Sample varies largely according to thickness of the yarn or size of the needle, and thickness of your knitting.

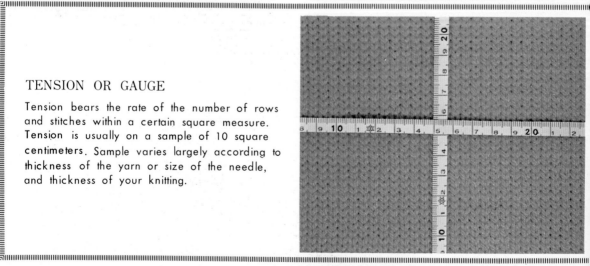

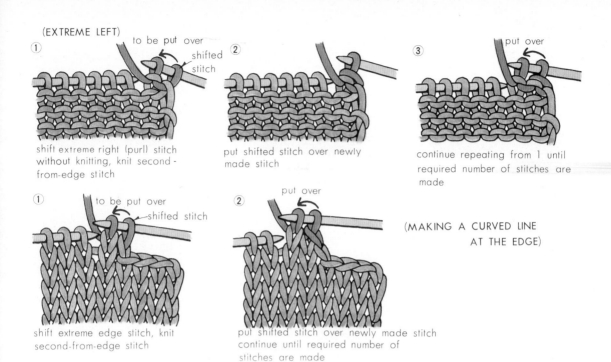

(EXTREME LEFT)

① to be put over / shifted stitch

shift extreme right (purl) stitch without knitting, knit second-from-edge stitch

② put shifted stitch over newly made stitch

③ put over

continue repeating from 1 until required number of stitches are made

① to be put over / shifted stitch

shift extreme edge stitch, knit second-from-edge stitch

② put over

put shifted stitch over newly made stitch continue until required number of stitches are made

(MAKING A CURVED LINE AT THE EDGE)

TO DECREASE IN THE COURSE OF KNITTING

(CLUSTER WITH RIGHT STITCH FRONT)

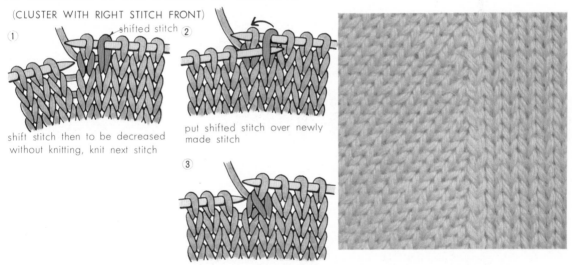

① shifted stitch

shift stitch then to be decreased without knitting, knit next stitch

② put shifted stitch over newly made stitch

③

SAMPLE SQUARE

Make foundation stitches to 15 cm in length using the yarn and needles you are going to make a piece with. Knit in the pattern stitching you're going to use for the work. Smooth the knit piece (15 square centimeters) with steam iron. Note: Some synthetic yarns require no ironing (if mentioned so) or certain low temperature (degree depends on the the type of the synthetic). Leave the sample for a while. Remeasure it.

CHECKING OF TENSION

It's not easy to measure the uneven surface of the knit piece— this is why ironing is essential. After smoothing the ribbed, raised, cabled or complicately designed stitches, place the piece on a flat. Count the rows and stitches in 10 cm square in center where they are made comparatively even.

(CLUSTER WITH LEFT STITCH FRONT)

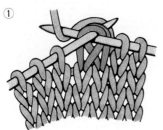

① 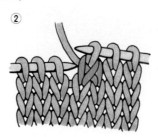 ②

work until 1 stitch before
stitch then to be decreased,
and 2 stitches together

||||||||||||||||||||||||||||||| TO INCREASE STITCHES |||||||||||||||||||||||||||||||||||||

Careful not to make increased stitches loose. If
increased on the edge, the stitches must be made
easy for later grafting. If increased in the course
of knitting, the stitches must be made in accord-
ance with the grain.

● TO INCREASE ON THE EDGE

(EXTREME RIGHT)

① stitch from second-from-top row   1 stitch newly made

② ③ newly increased

knit edge stitch, then needle
into second-from-top stitch
underneath, raise it to top

cast on, and knit

① (EXTREME LEFT)   stitch from 1 row under

edge stitch

② newly increased ③

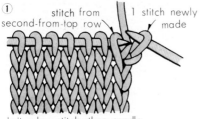

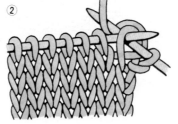

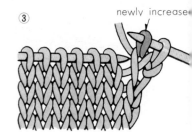

leave edge stitch unworked, insert
right needle in edge stitch previous
row, raise it to top, and knit.

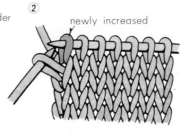

knit edge stitch

(LEFT)

(RIGHT)

● TO INCREASE 1 STITCH INSIDE THE EDGE

(EXTREME RIGHT)

①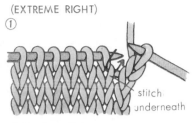

stitch underneath

knit edge stitch

②

insert right needle in second
but from previous row, cast
on yarn, and knit

③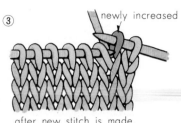

newly increased

after new stitch is made,
continue as usual

(EXTREME LEFT)

①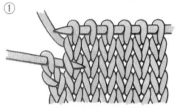

leave edge stitch unworked,
then left needle into neighboring
stitch that's second from top.

②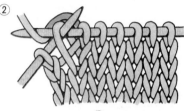

raise stitch ① and knit

③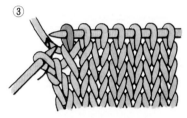

work edge stitch

PURL (EXTREME LEFT)

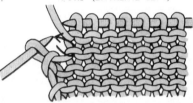

leave edge stitch unworked, left needle
neighboring stitch before previous row
(indicated), cast on yarn, and purl stitch

PURL (EXTREME RIGHT)

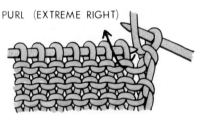

purl edge stitch, right needle into
neighboring stitch previous row,
cast on yarn, and purl stitch

(LEFT)  **(RIGHT)**

● TO INCREASE 2 STITCHES OR MORE ON THE EDGE

(EXTREME LEFT)

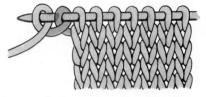

bring end of yarn toward you, casting
yarn on your left forefinger, put needle
through, and pull it forming a loop on
needle

(EXTREME RIGHT)

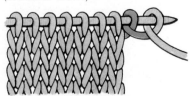

bring end of yarn toward you, casting
yarn on your right forefinger, put needle
through, and pull it forming a loop
on needle

35

You can either leave the edge stitches unworked or work in new stitches, to form a slanting edge such as shoulder slope or chest dart or curved

hem. Eliminating stitches every second row is common (shown in Stockinet Stitch).

● LEAVING EDGE STITCHES UNWORKED : ELIMINATION BY 2 ROWS

STOCKINET STITCH (KNIT SIDE FOR FRONT)

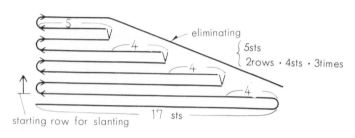

(RIGHT)

① 2nd row to be left unworked

complete 1st row, then leave 4 stitches (for example here) unworked at 2nd row

② 3rd row   to be shifted

turn right side up, shift 1 stitch onto right needle, and continue

③ 4th row

to be left unworked

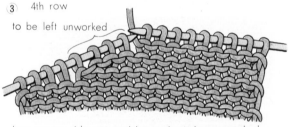

turn wrong side up, and leave 4 stitches unworked

④

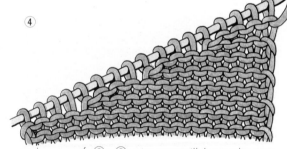

as in case of ②, ③ extra row will be made on side of yarn end

⑤ ELIMINATING THE ROW EDGES

scooping passed stitch on wrong side, exchange last two stitches

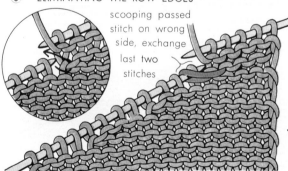

work with wrong side up, and where stitch shifted, exchange 2 stitches as shown, and work 2 stitches together.

⑥ COMPLETING THE SLOPE
(VIEW FROM
WRONG SIDE)

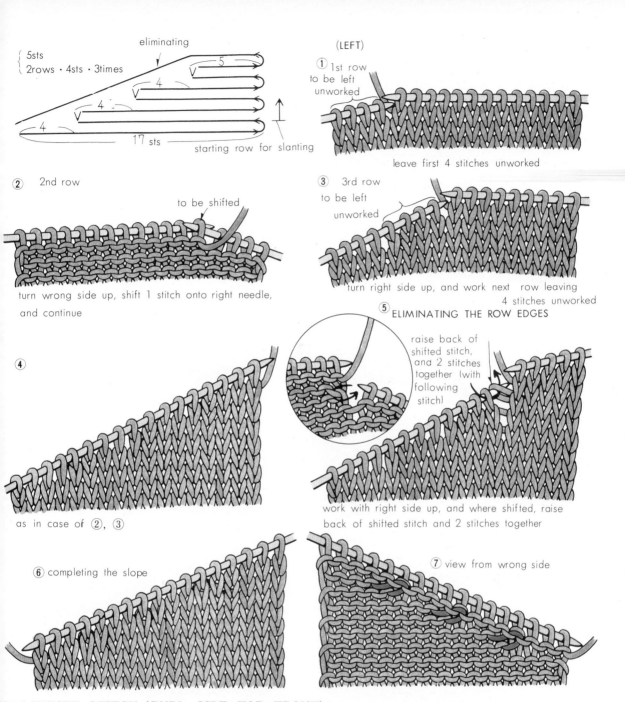

eliminating

5 sts
2 rows · 4 sts · 3 times

V 5
V 4
4
4

17 sts

starting row for slanting

(LEFT)

① 1st row to be left unworked

leave first 4 stitches unworked

② 2nd row

to be shifted

turn wrong side up, shift 1 stitch onto right needle, and continue

③ 3rd row to be left unworked

turn right side up, and work next row leaving 4 stitches unworked

④

as in case of ②, ③

⑤ ELIMINATING THE ROW EDGES

raise back of shifted stitch, and 2 stitches together (with following stitch)

work with right side up, and where shifted, raise back of shifted stitch and 2 stitches together

⑥ completing the slope

⑦ view from wrong side

STOCKINET STITCH (PURL SIDE FOR FRONT)

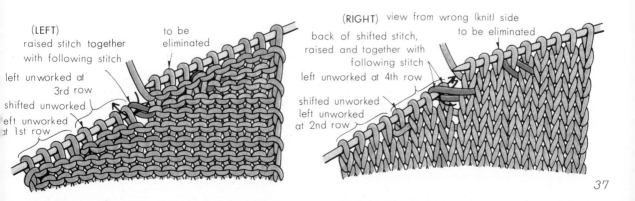

(LEFT)
raised stitch together with following stitch

to be eliminated

left unworked at 3rd row

shifted unworked

left unworked at 1st row

(RIGHT) view from wrong (knit) side

to be eliminated

back of shifted stitch, raised and together with following stitch

left unworked at 4th row

shifted unworked left unworked at 2nd row

STOCKINET STITCH (KNIT SIDE FOR FRONT)

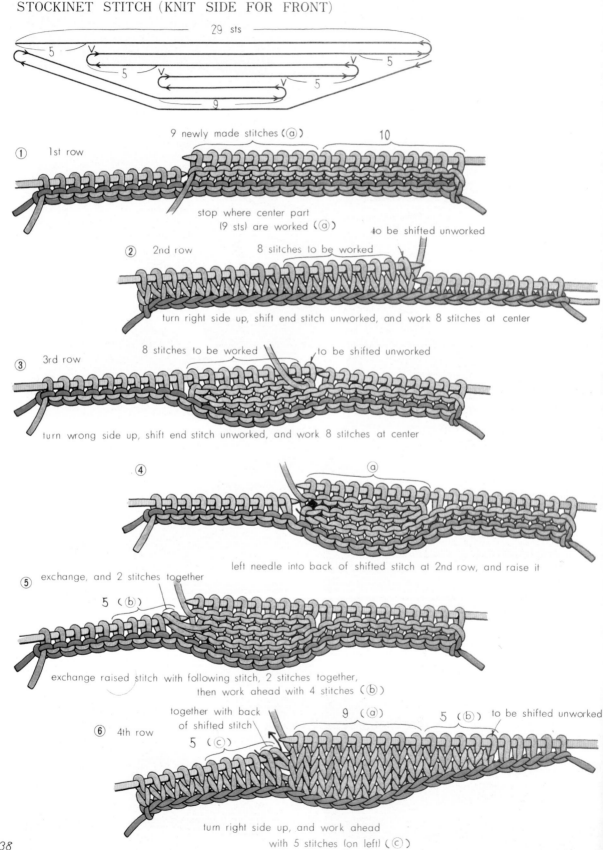

29 sts

5   V   5   V   5   V   5

9

① 1st row

9 newly made stitches (ⓐ)   10

stop where center part
(9 sts) are worked (ⓐ)

to be shifted unworked

② 2nd row   8 stitches to be worked

turn right side up, shift end stitch unworked, and work 8 stitches at center

③ 3rd row   8 stitches to be worked   to be shifted unworked

turn wrong side up, shift end stitch unworked, and work 8 stitches at center

④   ⓐ

left needle into back of shifted stitch at 2nd row, and raise it

⑤ exchange, and 2 stitches together

5 (ⓑ)

exchange raised stitch with following stitch, 2 stitches together,
then work ahead with 4 stitches (ⓑ)

together with back
of shifted stitch   9 (ⓐ)   5 (ⓑ)   to be shifted unworked

⑥ 4th row   5 (ⓒ)

turn right side up, and work ahead
with 5 stitches (on left) (ⓒ)

⑦ 5th row (1st row of regular stitching)

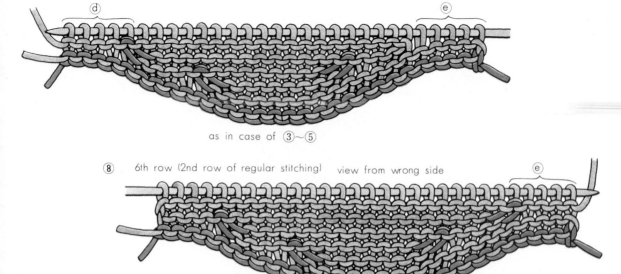

as in case of ③~⑤

⑧ 6th row (2nd row of regular stitching)   view from wrong side

IIIIIIIIIIIIIIIIIIIIIIIIIIIIIIIIIIIIIIII **TO FINISH THE EDGE** IIIIIIIIIIIIIIIIIIIIIIIIIIIIIIIIIIIIIIIIIIIIIIIIIII

With the piece worked in stockinet stitch with knit side front, you use the knitting needles you've used for the work. With the piece worked in stotckinet stitch with purl side front a crochet hook must be used to used to bind off the edge. And with a ribbed piece, a sewing needle for yarn will be applied. In any case, the yarn for edging should be 3 times as long as the actual length of the edge.

● **BINDING OFF**

STOCKINET STITCH WITH KNIT SIDE FOR FRONT

using the knitting needles

① to be shifted over

with stitch **1** on right needle, work stitch **2**, then with left needle stitch shift **1** over newly made stitch

③ bind off repeating from **1**

STOCKINET STITCH WITH PURL SIDE FOR FRONT

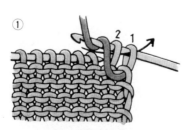

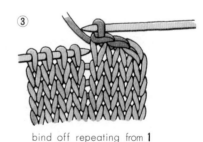

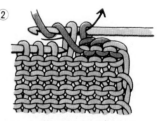

① with yarn on your side, hook into stitch **1** then into stitch **2**, cast on yarn, and pull three together

② bind off repeating from **1**

SINGLE-RIBBED

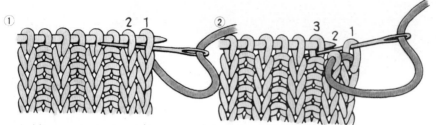

holding yarn on your right,
needle into stitches **1** and **2**
as shown

back to stitch **1**, needle from front,
and emerge on wrong side through
stitch **3**

SINGLE RIB BIND-OFF

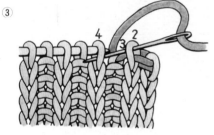

back to stitch **2**, needle into through
to stitch **4**, skipping stitch **3**, emerging
on right side.

DOUBLE RIB BIND-OFF

DOUBLE-RIBBED

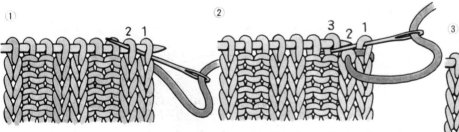

with yarn on your right, needle
into stitches **1** and **2** as shown,
emerging on right side

back to stitch **1**, needle into through
to stitch **3**, skipping stitch **2**, emerging
on wrong side

needle into stitch **2** from right side,
through to stitch **5**, skipping stitches
3 and **4**, emerging on right side

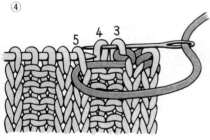

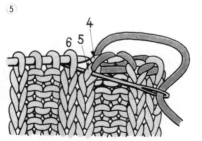

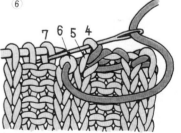

back to stitch **3**, needle into from
wrong side, emerging through
stitch **4**

needle into stitch **5** from right
side, and emerges through
stitch **6** from wrong side

needle into stitch **4** from wrong
side, through to **7**, skipping stitches
5 and **6**
continue joining 2 stitches at one time

There are several methods to work pattern stitching, and they vary according to the type of pattern used for your garment. In case decorative yarns are knitted in a basic yarn, the yarns should be passed under on the wrong side. In case, however, decorative yarns are crowdedly used such as in a diamond motif, the yarns should be mitered as shown in the illustrations.

● PATTERN STITCHINGS

PASSING UNDER THE YARNS

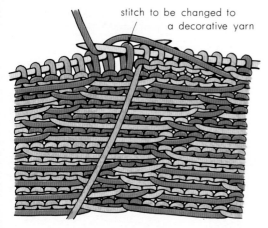

stitch to be changed to a decorative yarn

when you change to decorative yarn, knit pattern stitching with decorative yarn, leaving basic yarn unworked and passed under flat as shown here

MITERING THE YARNS

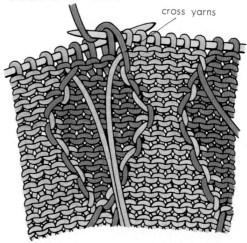

cross yarns

work as in case of vertical stripe stitching, crossing basic yarn with decorative at border.

WITH THE YARNS PASSED UNDER (RIGHT SIDE)

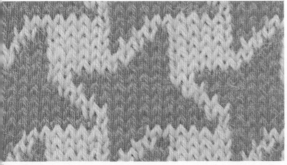

(WRONG SIDE)

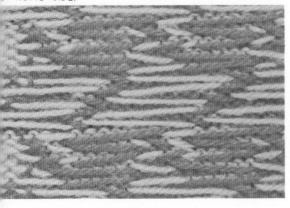

WITH THE YARNS MITERED (RIGHT SIDE)

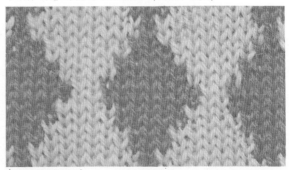

(WRONG SIDE)

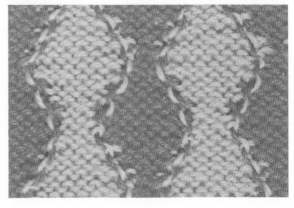

HORIZONTAL STRIPE

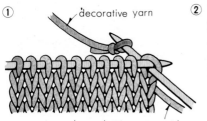

① decorative yarn

② basic yarn

leave basic yarn aside

leave basic yarn unworked at edge, draw out decorative yarn through 1st stitch and work on in regular stitching

when change to basic yarn, leave decorative yarn on your side, bring basic yarn on wrong side, then start in regular stitching (careful not to pull yarns)

decorative yarn

HORIZONTAL STRIPE (RIGHT SIDE)

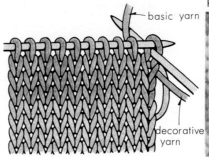

(WRONG SIDE)

VERTICAL STRIPE

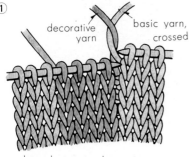

① decorative yarn

basic yarn, crossed

②

when change to decorative yarn, cross it with basic yarn so that be finished neatly

when change to basic yarn, cross it with decorative yarn for same reason as ①

view on wrong side of piece

crossed

VERTICAL STRIPE (RIGHT SIDE)

(WRONG SIDE)

WHEN THE YARN IS RUNNING SHORT HALFWAY OF WORK

Better not to link with a new yarn in the course of the row, but tie with the new one at the edge of the row. Leave the end of the new yarn (4-5cm) at the edge untied, to be tied with the old later. The both ends will be sewn in a margin.

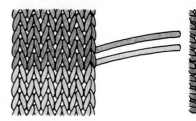

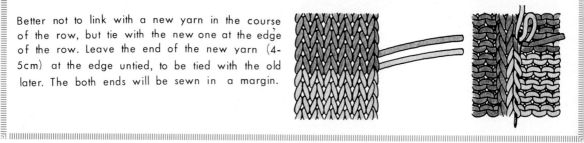

GRATING (ASSEMBLING THE PIECES)

Some graftings are aimed at giving elasticity, while others at allowing no stretch.

● STOCKINET STITCH (KNIT SIDE FOR FRONT)

WITH STITCHES LEFT ON THE NEEDLES

Difference in the direction of the stitches of the two pieces naturally causes a half-stitch shift in linking, yet this is a method that provides enough elasticity and invisible seam.

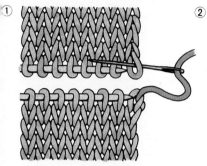

① needle inserted from back emerges on front through farther edge stitch

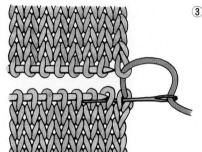

② back to nearer edge stitch, re-inserted front emerges on back through next stitch

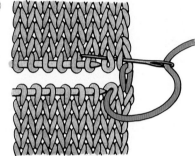

③ needle re-inserted into 1st stitch from front emerges on through next stitch from back

● GARTER STITCH

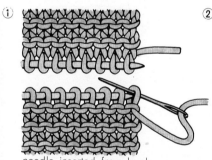

① needle inserted from back emerges on front through nearer edge stitch

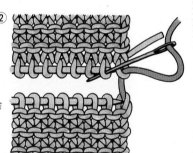

② needle emerged from back of farther edge stitch, emerges on back through 2nd farther stitch

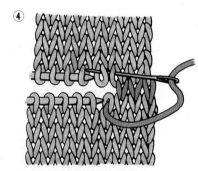

④ repeat from ②, ③

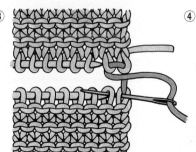

③ back to nearer edge stitch, re-inserted, emerges on front from back

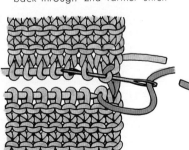

④ needle emerged on front through 2nd farther stitch, emerges on back through front of 3rd stitch. repeat from ②, ③ making nearer stitches liked on front and farther stitches on back

⑤

TO CONNECT STITCHES WITH ROWS

This method of making up needs previous check of the tension in stitches and rows. In case of stockinet-stitched pieces, 3 stitches are to be sewn to 4 rows.

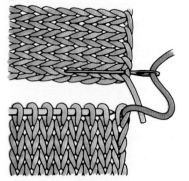

①

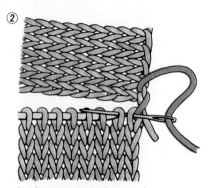

②

③

needle emerges from back of farther edge stitch

back to nearer edge stitch, needle in from front, then it comes out through next stitch

continue, scooping sinker loop between edge row and second row of upper piece, to connect with top stitches of lower piece

‖‖‖‖‖‖‖ **TO SEW UP STRAIGHT** ‖‖‖‖‖‖‖‖‖

STOCKINET STITCH PIECES
SCOOPING SINKER LOOPS IN EVERY ROW

This method is frequently used for making up stockinet stitch pieces. Put out the yarn at either every row or every second row, or, with thicker yarns, sew up by connecting every half of the edge stitches.

TO SEW UP SLANTWISE

place two pieces with right sides up and edge to edge, then scoop edge stitches one by one

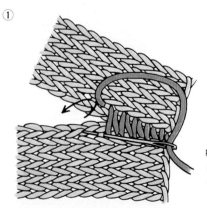

①

place two pieces with right sides up and edge to edge, and scoop sinker loops along side the edges

②

HOW TO LINK WITH A NEW YARN IN THE COURSE OF WORK

Leave the yarn end in 4-5 cm in the course. Continue working with a new yarn without tying its end.
Both ends will be then finished as illustrated.

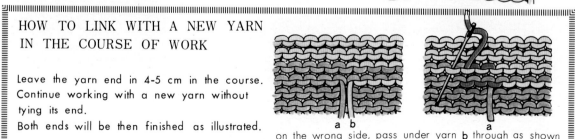

a b   a
on the wrong side, pass under yarn **b** through as shown

IN SLIP STITCH

This method is used to protect the sewn-up part from loosening.

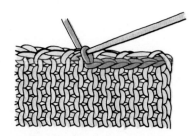

join two pieces with right sides together, insert hook in second-from-edge stitch, draw yarn through over lapped pieces at every row

IN BACK STITCH

This method is used to keep raised surface of the knitted piece neat (usually it's loose at edge) Insert the needle almost perpendicularly so that stitches won't become irregular.

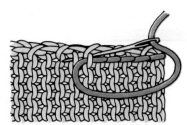

join two pieces with right sides together, scoop 2 vertical loops at next-to-edge rows, and sew up in backstitch

● STOCKINET STITCH WITH PURL SIDE FRONT

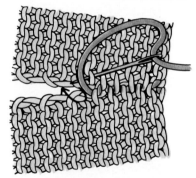

place two pieces with purl sides up, edge to edge, and scoop first lower stitch from next-to-edge row of upper piece, then higher stitch from corresponding row of lower piece. repeat alternately

● GARTER

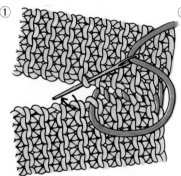

① plase two pieces with right sides up, edge to edge, and scoop lower half of edge stitch of upper piece, then upper half of edge stitch of lower piece

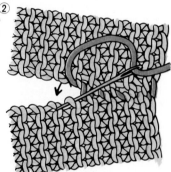

② thus repeated alternately, garter stitches are linked correctly

● SINGLE RIBBED, WITH ONE EDGE DOUBLE-RIBBED

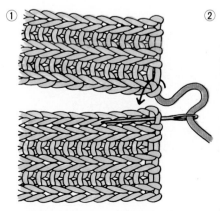

① place right sides up and needle into edge, knit stitch at bottom then second from bottom sinker loop

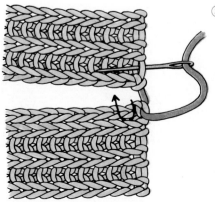

② needle into upper piece at bottom purl stitch then second sinker loop

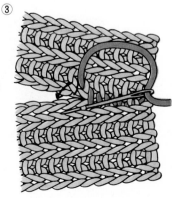

③ repeat alternately

45

● SEWING IN SLIP STITCH

This method is made by scooping the upper half of edge stitch (horizontal chain) and connecting it with the lower half of the purl stitch (wrong side) with 1 row shifted.

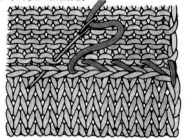

make sewing stitches rather loose
that be invisible on front. if yarn
is thick, split in two and use one half

● WORKING KNIT-PURL STITCHES NEWLY

Knit and purl stitches are made newly while fini-shing hem. This method is often used for finishing neckline or front facing.

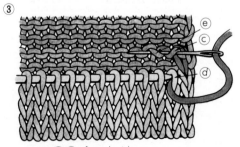

① needle from back of edge stitch ⓐ to scoop ⓑⓒ of purl side

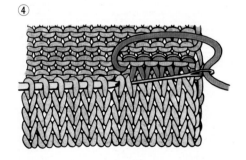

② back to ⓐ, needle through ⓐ and comes out from back of ⓓ

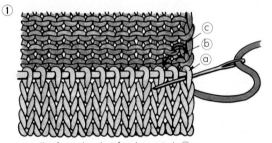

③ scoop ⓒⓔ of purl side
repeat from ②

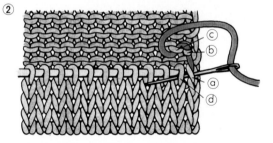

④

TO PICK OUT STITCHES

Measure the desired length in advance, then make sure of the necessary number of stitches to ~e then picked out.

● PICKING OUT FROM THE ROWS

With a crochet hook, or a knitting needle (illus-
~ated), pick out in ratio of 3 stitches for 4 rows.

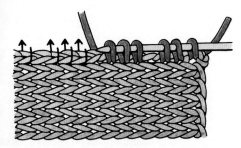

needle into between 1st and 2nd stitches
of knit side, and pull separate yarn through

needle into between 1st and 2nd stitches
of purl side, and pull separate yarn through

● PICKING OUT FROM CURVED EDGE

Neckline

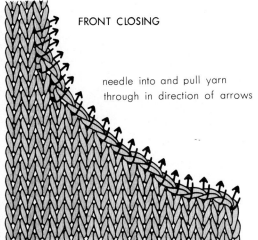

FRONT CLOSING

needle into and pull yarn
through in direction of arrows

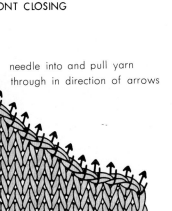

When you pick out stitches from a curved edge, such as neckline or armhole, the ratio of 3 stitches for 4 rows may be used for vertical part of the curve and 1 stitch for 1 row for horizontal part of the curve.
When you pick out stitches from a symmetrically curved edge, such as neckline of pullover, pick out stitches from corresponding rows right and left.

PULL'S NECKLINE

needle into and yarn through
as indicated by arrows

pick out stitch by stitch where
stitches are left unedged

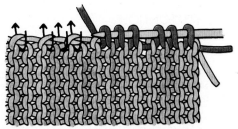

‖‖‖‖‖‖‖‖‖‖‖‖‖‖‖‖‖‖‖‖‖‖ TO MAKE BUTTONHOLES ‖‖‖‖‖‖‖‖‖‖‖‖‖‖‖‖‖‖‖‖‖‖

You can make buttonholes while working, or make them later. Important is the size and location of them.

● **SMALL BUTTONHOLE**

diagram

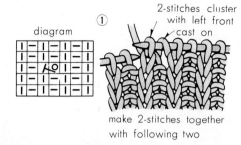

① 2-stitches cluster with left front cast on

make 2-stitches together with following two

② continue as before trim the edge later, if necessa

● **SPLIT BUTTONHOLE**

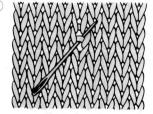

① put needle in location, and pull up under loop of stitch

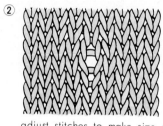

② adjust stitches to make size of button

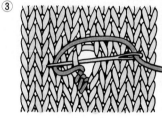

③ trim edge with separate yarn in same color on right side

● **VERTICAL BUTTONHOLE**

when you come to location of buttonhole divide stitches right and left, and work one half as long as button's diameter attach yarn newly on left-aside half, work 2-stitches together to begin with, and continue to length of former half

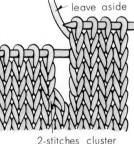

① leave aside

2-stitches cluster with left front

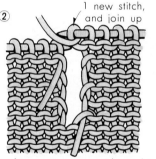

② 1 new stitch, and join up

when work wrong side, make a new stitch, join two pieces as shown, and work on in one piece

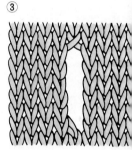

③ if necessary, trim edge c right side

● **HORIZONTAL BUTTONHOLE**

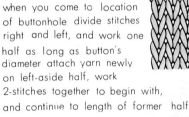

① to be shifted over to be shifted

when you come to location of buttonhole, shift 1 stitch unworked, work next stitch, then put shifted stitch over new stitch

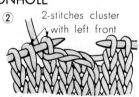

② 2-stitches cluster with left front

shift stitches over to length of button's diameter, and work 2 stitches cluster with left front for last

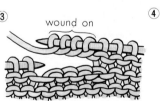

③ wound on

while working next row, wind on as many time as number of skipped stitches

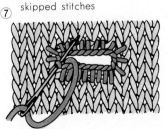

④

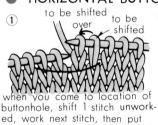

⑤ split yarn in two, and work buttonhole edge with

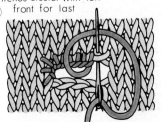

⑥ edge on right side of piece

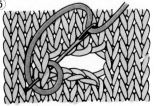

⑦ make one round in open buttonhole stitch, and end on wrong side